WHEEL AWAY!

by **Dayle Ann Dodds**

illustrations by **Thacher Hurd**

Harper & Row, Publishers

Wheel Away!

Text copyright © 1989 by Dayle Ann Dodds

Illustrations copyright © 1989 by Thacher Hurd

Printed in the U.S.A. All rights reserved.

1 2 3 4 5 6 7 8 9 10

First Edition

Library of Congress Cataloging-in-Publication Data

Dodds, Dayle Ann.

   Wheel away!

   Summary: A runaway wheel takes a bouncy, bumpy,
amusing journey through town.

   [1. Wheels—Fiction.   2. Stories in rhyme]

I. Hurd, Thacher, ill.   II. Title.

PZ8.3.D645Wh 1989   [E]   87-27091

ISBN 0-06-021688-3

ISBN 0-06-021689-1 (lib. bdg.)

For Glen, Jaime, and Greg
D.D.

For Manton
T.H.

Oh no! See it go!

pa-da-rump

pa-da-rump

pa-da-rump-pump-pump

bump

Down the hill

bump

bump

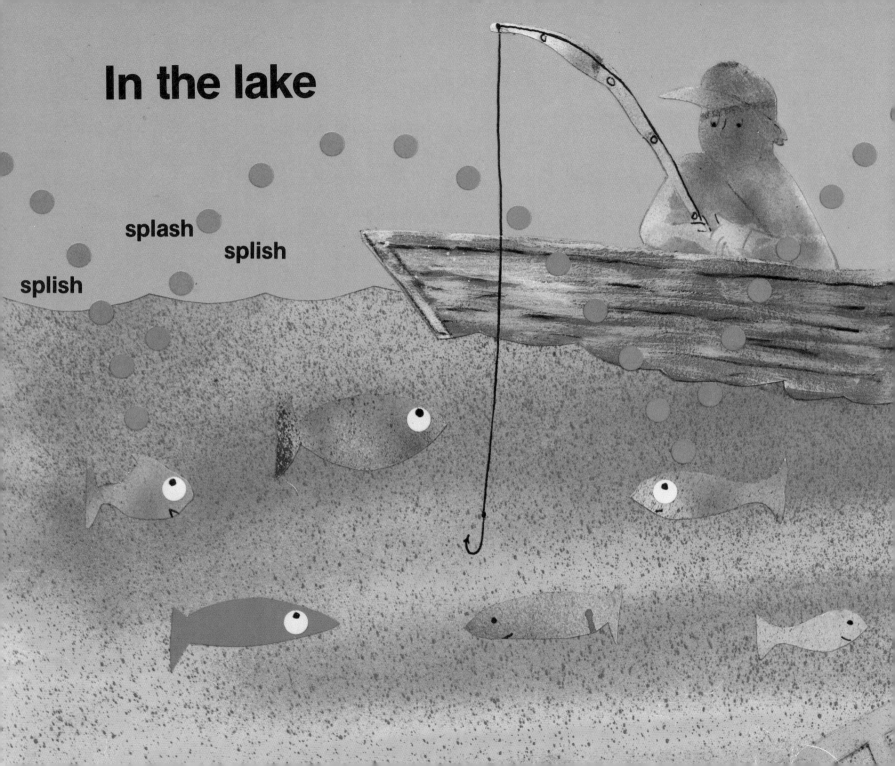

In the lake

splash

splish

splish

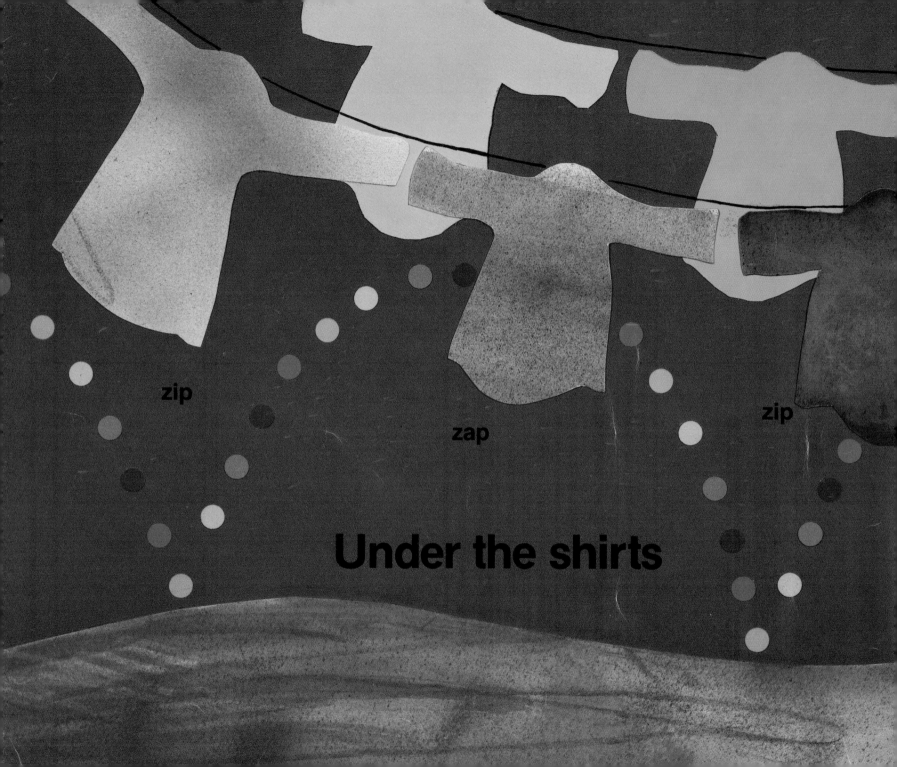

zip

zap

zip

Under the shirts

whip

whap

whip

Across the dirt

Between the pens

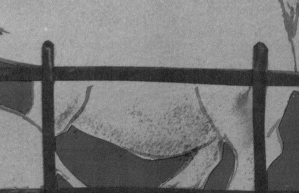

oink

oink

oink

On top of the hens

boink

boink

boink

Oh no! On it goes!

pa-da-rump   pa-da-rump   pa-da-rump-pump-pump

On new road tar

bop

bop

bop

Past church bazaar

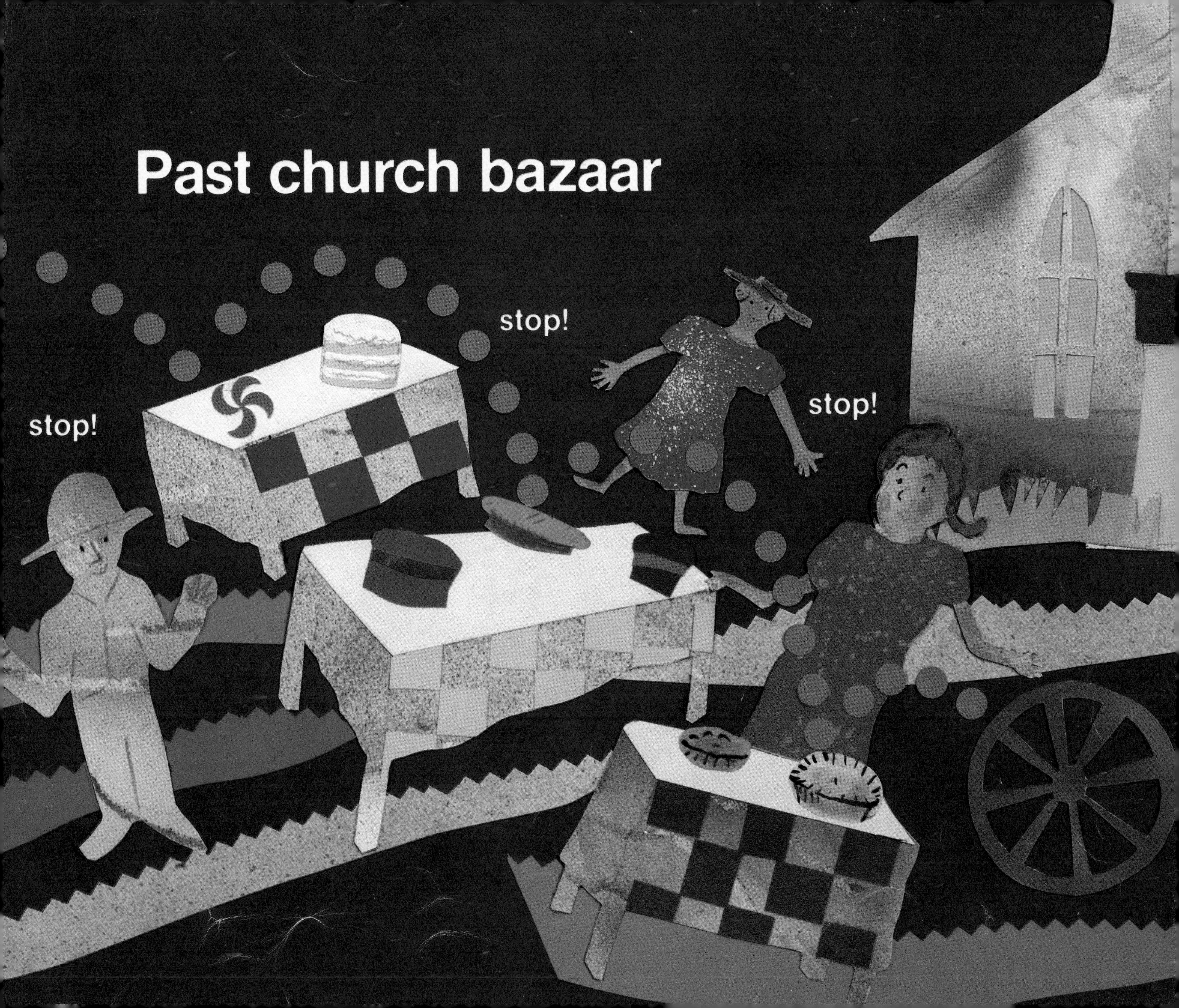

Over paint cans

squirt

squirt

squirt

Under paint man

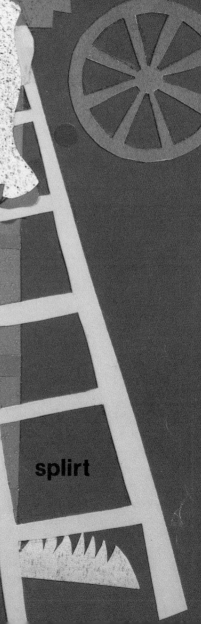

splirt

splirt

splirt

In front of the truck

clickety-clack

In back of the duck

quackety-quack

Oh no! See it go!

pa-da-rump   pa-da-rump

pa-da-rump-pump-pump

climbing

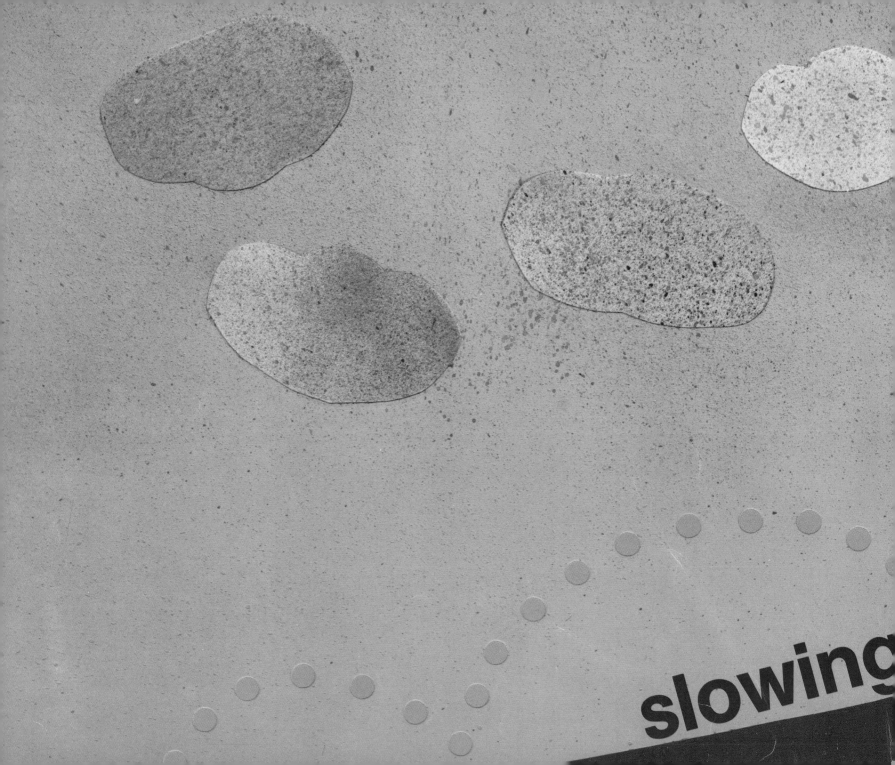

slowing

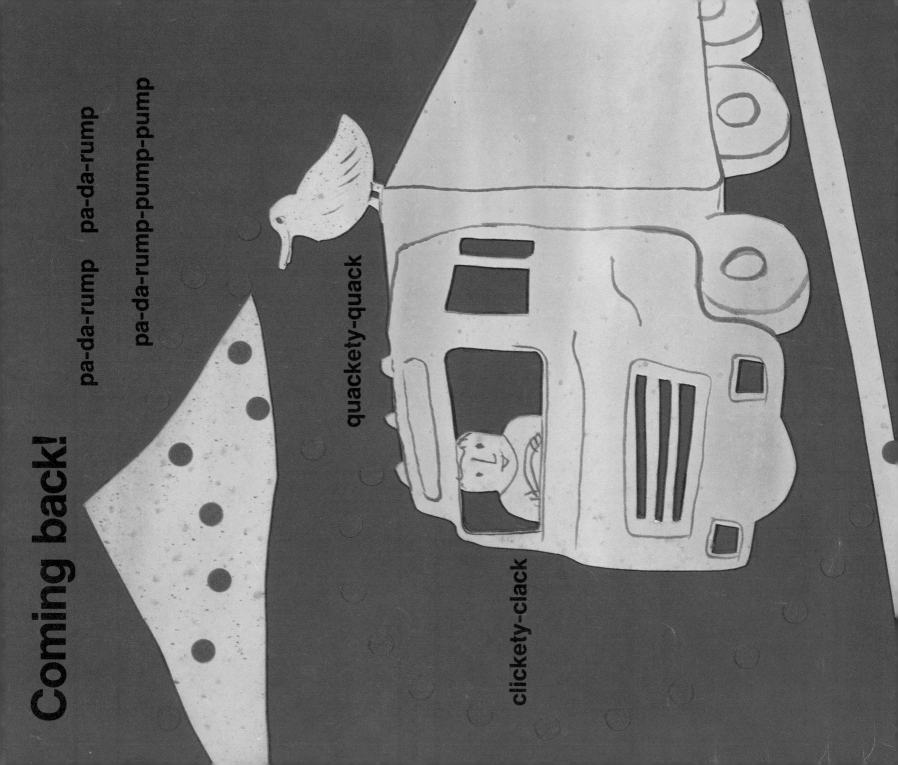

Coming back!

pa-da-rump   pa-da-rump

pa-da-rump-pump-pump

quackety-quack

clickety-clack

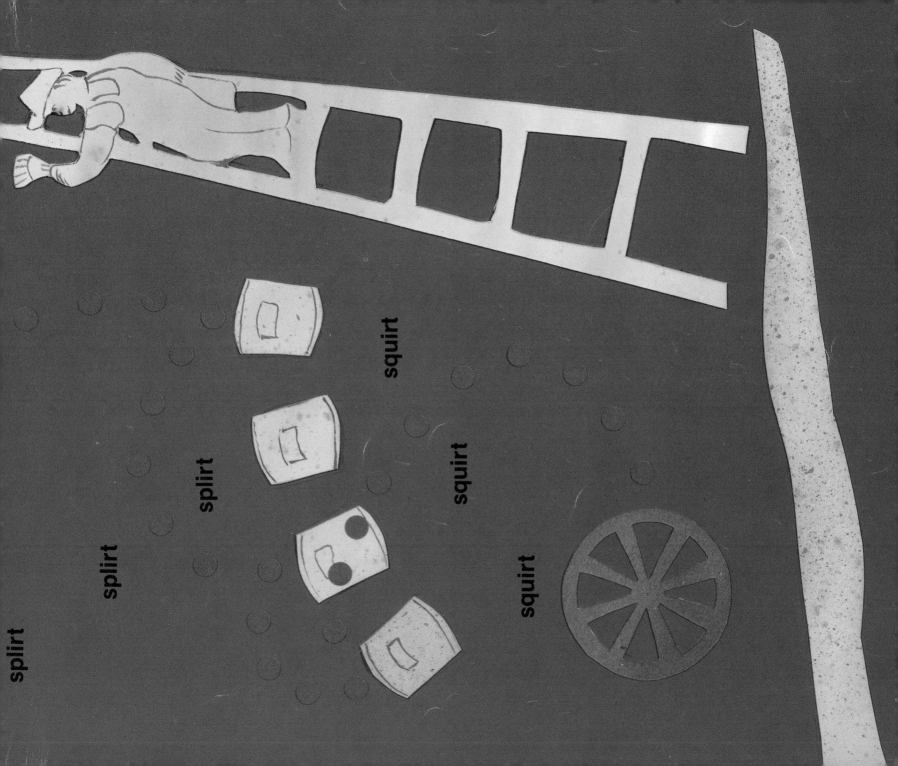

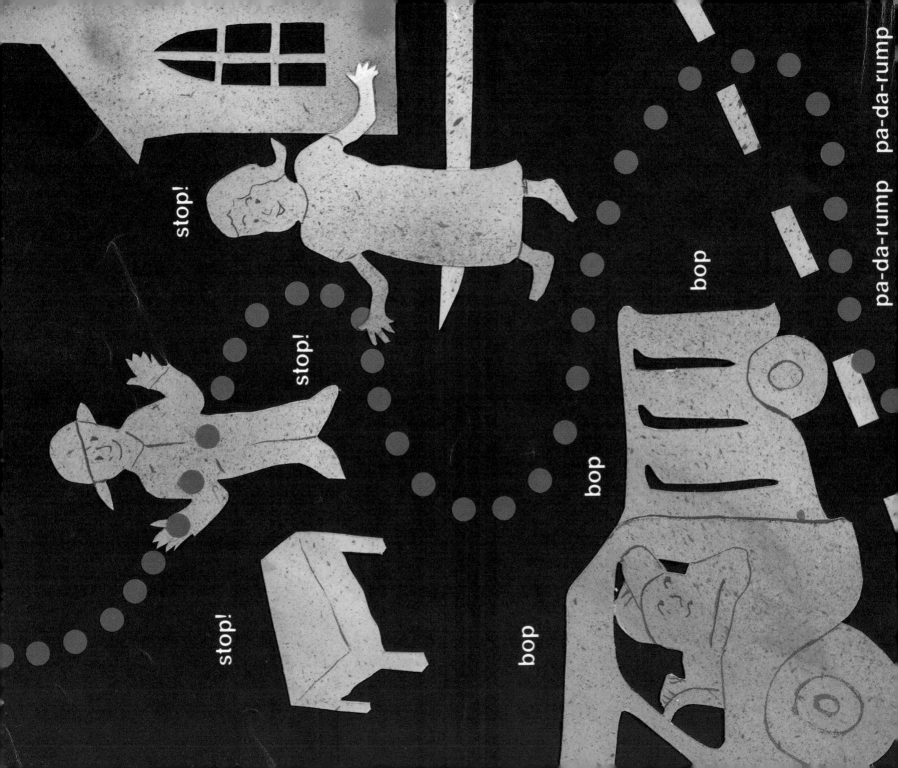

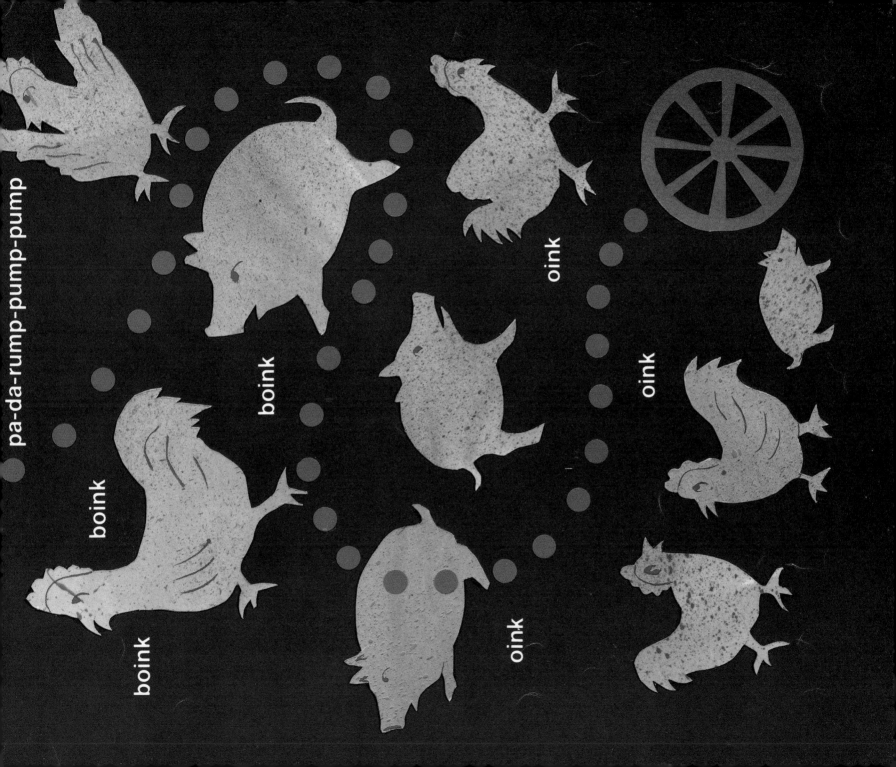

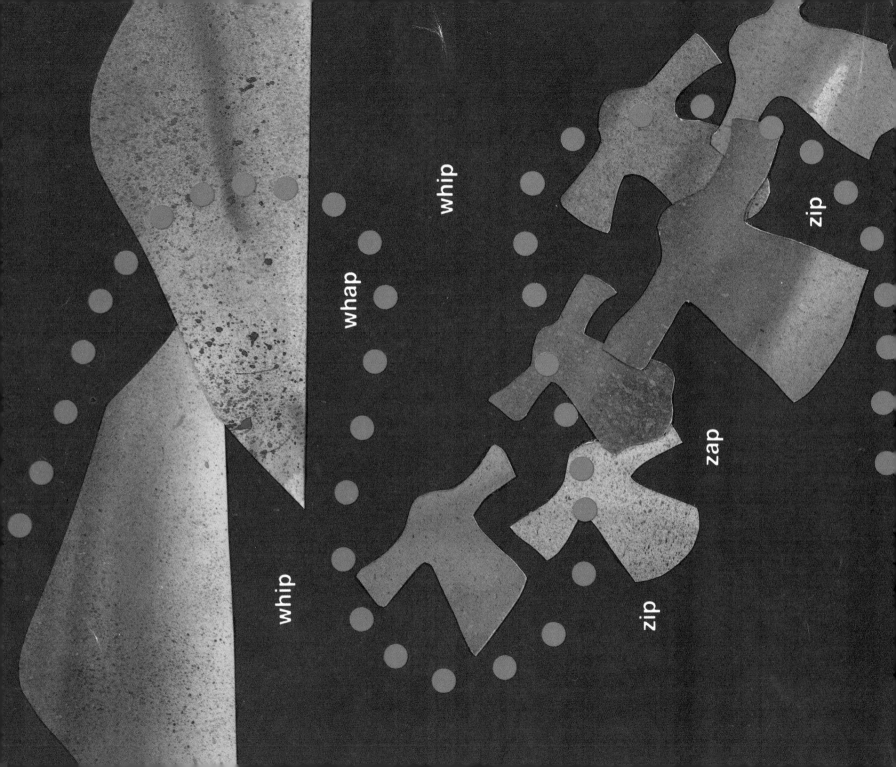

whip

whap

whip

zip

zap

zip

whip

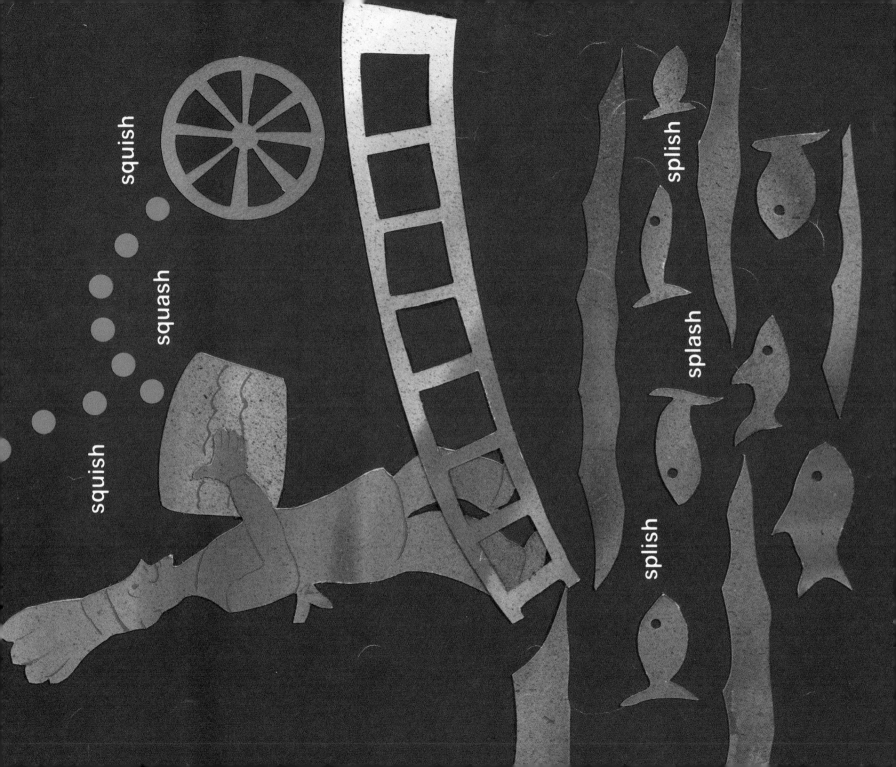

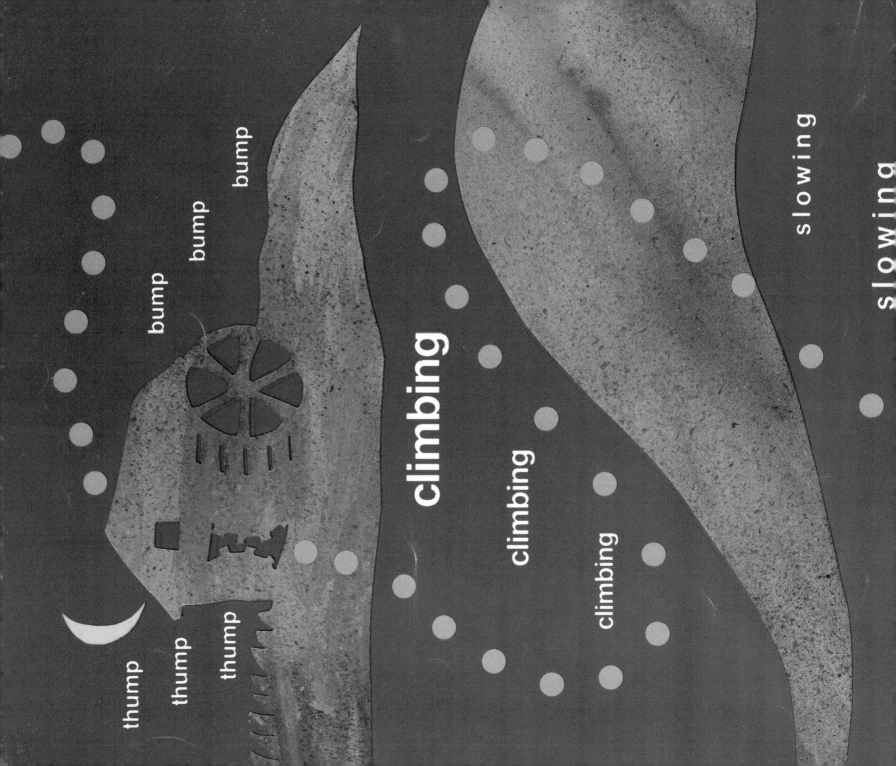